Theosophical Basics

By
William Q. Judge

Copyright © 2022 Lamp of Trismegistus. All rights reserved. No part of this publication may be reproduced or transmitted in any form or by any means, electronic or mechanical, including photocopying, recording, or by any information storage and retrieval system, without permission in writing from Lamp of Trismegistus. Reviewers may quote brief passages.

ISBN: 978-1-63118-608-0

Esoteric Classics

Other Books in this Series and Related Titles

Aurora of the Philosophers by Paracelsus (978-1-63118-507-6)

Rosicrucian Rules, Secret Signs, Codes and Symbols by various (978-1-63118-488-8)

On the Philadelphian Gold by Philochrysus & Philadelphus (978-1-63118-511-3)

Paracelsus, the Four Elements and Their Spirits by M P Hall (978-1-63118-400-0)

The Stone of the Philosophers by A E Waite (978-1-63118-509-0)

Clairvoyance and Psychic Abilities by A Besant &c (978-1-63118-403-1)

The Rosicrucian Chemical Marriage by Christian Rosenkreuz (978-1-63118-458-1)

The Alchemical Catechism of Paracelsus by Paracelsus (978-1-63118-513-7)

Alchemy in the Nineteenth Century by Helena P. Blavatsky (978-1-63118-446-8)

Rosicrucians and Speculative Masonry in the Seventeenth Century (978-1-63118-489-5)

Qabbalistic Teachings and the Tree of Life by M P Hall (978-1-63118-482-6)

The Sepher Yetzirah and the Qabalah by M P Hall (978-1-63118-481-9)

The Devil in Love by Jacques Cazotte (978–1–63118–499–4)

Fortune-Telling with Dice by Astra Cielo (978-1-63118-466-6)

History, Analysis and Secret Tradition of the Tarot by Hall &c (978-1-63118-445-1)

Crystal Vision Through Crystal Gazing by Frater Achad (978-1-63118-455-0)

The Golden Verses of Pythagoras: Five Translations (978-1-63118-479-6)

Arcane Formulas or Mental Alchemy by W W Atkinson (978-1-63118-459-8)

The Machinery of the Mind by Dion Fortune (978-1-63118-451-2)

The A E Waite Reader: A Selection of Occult Essays (978-1-63118-515-1)

The Leadbeater Reader: A Selection of Occult Essays (978-1-63118-483-3)

Audio versions are also available on Audible, Amazon and Apple

Other Books in this Series and Related Titles

The Hebrew Talisman by Richard Harte (978–1–63118–607–3)

Early Masonic Symbolism by Manly P Hall (978–1–63118–606–6)

Nature Spirits and Elementals by Louise Off (978-1-63118-605-9)

Swedenborg Bifrons by H P Blavatsky (978-1-63118-604-2)

Practical Use of Psychic Powers by C W Leadbeater (978-1-63118-603-5)

Using White & Black Magic by C W Leadbeater (978-1-63118-602-8)

Jesus, the Last Great Initiate by Edouard Schure (978-1-63118-599-1)

Mysterious Wonders of Antiquity by Manly P Hall (978-1-63118-598-4)

Ancient Mysteries and Secret Societies by Manly P Hall (978–1–63118–597–7)

The Zodiac and Its Signs by Manly P Hall (978–1–63118–596–0)

Life and Teachings of Hermes Trismegistus by Manly P Hall (978–1–63118–595–3)

The Secrets of Doctor Taverner by Dion Fortune (978–1–63118–594–6)

Vegetarianism, Theosophy & Occultism by Leadbeater &c (978–1–63118–593–9)

Applied Theosophy by Henry S Olcott (978–1–63118–592–2)

Higher Consciousness by C W Leadbeater (978–1–63118–591–5)

Theories About Reincarnation and Spirits by H P Blavatsky (978–1–63118–590–8)

The Use and Power of Thought by C W Leadbeater (978–1–63118–589–2)

Commentary on the Pymander by G R S Mead (978–1–63118–588–5)

Hypnotism and Mesmerism by Annie Besant (978–1–63118–587–8)

Spirits of Various Kinds by Helena P Blavatsky (978–1–63118–586–1)

The Hidden Language of Symbolism by Annie Besant (978–1–63118–585–4)

Audio versions are also available on Audible, Amazon and Apple

Table of Contents

Introduction...7

Epitome of Theosophical Teachings...9

What Are Theosophists?...28

Theosophical Concepts of Evolution and Religion...30

What is the Theosophical Society?...54

INTRODUCTION

The word "esoteric" can be difficult to define. Esotericism in general can be seen less as a system of beliefs and more as a category, which encompasses numerous, different systems of beliefs. It's a bit of juxtaposition, since the word "esoteric" indicates something that few people know about, while the term itself broadly covers numerous philosophies, practices, areas of study and belief systems.

In a greater sense, Esotericism acts as a storehouse for secret knowledge, which is often considered ancient (by *tradition, if not by fact*), passed down from generation to generation, in private. At various times in history, simply possessing the knowledge of some of these subjects, was considered illegal and a jailable offence, if discovered. This usually included such general topics as Alchemy, Pharmacology, Qabalah, Hermeticism, Occultism, Ceremonial Magic, Astrology, Divination, Rosicrucianism and so on. Collectively, these areas of study were often referred to as the esoteric sciences.

Sometimes, the outer garment of a subject isn't esoteric, while what is hidden beneath it, is. As an example, Freemasonry isn't necessarily esoteric by nature (at *least not anymore)*, but certain signs, passwords and handshakes given to the candidate during their initiation, are in fact, esoteric, in the sense that they are hidden from the general public.

Today, in the twenty-first century, such topics are readily available at bookstores across the country, and numerous main-steam publishers offer beginners guides and coffee-table volumes on many of these subjects, intended for mass appeal. Books like *"The Secret"* have turned previously arcane topics into household knowledge. All that being the case, however, it isn't to say that there still aren't buried secrets to uncover, ancient wisdom being ignored and forgotten mysteries to be explored. In fact, it is often that we are only able to further our own studies by standing on the shoulders of these disappearing giants.

Lamp of Trismegistus is doing its part to help preserve humanity's esoteric history by making some of these classics available to those students who are seeking to unearth the knowledge of these ancient colossi.

So, be sure to check other titles from our *Esoteric Classics* series, as well as our *Occult Fiction, Theosophical Classics, Foundations of Freemasonry Series, Supernatural Fiction, Paranormal Research Series, Studies in Buddhism* and our *Christian Apocrypha Series.* You can also download the audio versions of most of these titles from Amazon, Apple or Audible, for learning on the go.

EPITOME OF THEOSOPHICAL TEACHINGS

THEOSOPHY, the Wisdom-Religion, has existed from immemorial time. It offers us a theory of nature and of life which is founded upon knowledge acquired by the Sages of the past, more especially those of the East; and its higher students claim that this knowledge is not imagined or inferred, but that it is a knowledge of facts seen and known by those who are willing to comply with the conditions requisite for seeing and knowing.

Theosophy, meaning knowledge of or about God, [Not in the sense of a personal anthropomorphic God, but in that of divine "godly" wisdom.] and the term "God" being universally accepted as including the whole of both the known and the unknown, it follows that "Theosophy" must imply wisdom respecting the absolute; and, since the absolute is without beginning and eternal, this wisdom must have existed always. Hence Theosophy is sometimes called the Wisdom-Religion, because from immemorial time it has had knowledge of all the laws governing the spiritual, the moral, and the material.

The theory of nature and of life which it offers is not one that was at first speculatively laid down and then proved by adjusting facts or conclusions to fit it; but is an explanation of existence, cosmic and individual, derived from knowledge reached by those who have acquired the power to see behind the curtain that hides the operations of nature from the ordinary mind. Such Beings are called Sages, using the term in its highest sense. Of late they have been called Mahatmas and Adepts. In ancient times they were known as the Rishees and Maharishis, the last being a word that means Great Rishees.

It is not claimed that these exalted beings, or Sages, have existed only in the East. They are known to have lived in all parts of the globe, in obedience to the cyclic laws referred to below. But as far as concerns the present development of the human race on this planet, they now are to be found in the East, although the fact may be that some of them had, in remote times, retreated from even the American shores.

There being of necessity various grades among the students of this wisdom-religion, it stands to reason that those belonging to the lower degrees are able to give out only so much of the knowledge as is the appanage of the grade they have reached, and depend, to some extent, for further information upon students who are higher yet. It is these higher students for whom the claim is asserted that their knowledge is not mere inference, but that it concerns realities seen and known by them. While some of them are connected with the Theosophical Society, they are yet above it. The power to see and absolutely know such laws is surrounded by natural inherent regulations which must be complied with as conditions precedent; and it is, therefore, not possible to respond to the demand of the worldly man for an immediate statement of this wisdom, insomuch as he could not comprehend it until those conditions are fulfilled. As this knowledge deals with laws and states of matter, and of consciousness undreamed of by the "practical" western world, it can only be grasped, piece by piece, as the student pushes forward the demolition of his preconceived notions, that are due either to inadequate or to erroneous theories. It is claimed by these higher students that, in the Occident especially, a false method of reasoning has for many centuries prevailed, resulting in a universal habit of mind which causes men to look upon many effects as causes, and to regard that which is real as the unreal, putting meanwhile the unreal in the place of the real. As a minor example, the phenomena of mesmerism and clairvoyance, have, until lately, been denied by western science, yet there have always been numerous persons who know for themselves, by incontrovertible introspective evidence, the truth of these phenomena, and, in some instances, understand their cause and rationales.

The following are some of the fundamental propositions of Theosophy:—

The spirit in man is the only real and permanent part of his being; the rest of his nature being variously compounded. And since decay is incident to all composite things, everything in man but his spirit is impermanent.

Further, the universe being one thing and not diverse, and everything within it being connected with the whole and with every other thing therein, of which upon the upper plane (below referred to) there is a perfect knowledge, no act or thought occurs without each portion of the great whole perceiving and noting it. Hence all are inseparably bound together by the tie of Brotherhood.

This first fundamental proposition of Theosophy postulates that the universe is not an aggregation of diverse unities but that it is one whole. This whole is what is denominated "Deity" by Western Philosophers, and "Para-Brahm" by the Hindu Vedantins. It may be called the Unmanifested, containing within itself the potency of every form of manifestation, together with the laws governing those manifestations. Further, it is taught that there is no creation of worlds in the theological sense; but that their appearance is due strictly to evolution. When the time comes for the Unmanifested to manifest as an objective Universe, which it does periodically, it emanates a Power or "The First Cause", so called because it itself is the rootless root of that Cause, and called in the East the "Causeless Cause". The first Cause, we may call Brahmâ, or Ormazd, or Osiris, or by any name we please. The projection into time of the influence or so-called "breath of Brahmâ" causes all the worlds and the beings upon them to gradually appear. They remain in manifestation just as long as that influence continues to proceed forth in evolution. After long aeons the outbreathing, evolutionary influence slackens, and the universe begins to go into obscuration, or pralaya, until, the "breath" being fully indrawn, no objects remain, because nothing *is* but Brahma. Care must be taken by the student to make a distinction between Brahma (the impersonal Parabrahma) and Brahmâ the manifested Logos. A discussion of the means used by this power in acting would be out of place in this Epitome, but of those means Theosophy also treats.

This breathing-forth is known as a Manvantara, or the Manifestation of the world between two Manus (from Manu, and Antara "between") and the completion of the inspiration brings with it Pralaya, or destruction. It is from these truths that the erroneous doctrines of "creation" and the "last judgment" have sprung. Such Manvantaras and Pralayas have eternally occurred, and will continue to take place periodically, and for ever.

For the purpose of a manvantara two so-called eternal principles are postulated, that is, Purusha and Prakriti (or spirit and matter), because both are ever present and conjoined in each manifestation. Those terms are used here because no equivalent for them exists in English. Purusha is called "spirit", and Prakriti "matter", but this Purusha is not the unmanifested, nor is Prakriti matter as known to science; the Aryan Sages therefore declare that there is a higher spirit still, called Purushottama. The reason for this is that at the night of Brahma, or the so-called indrawing of his breath, both Purusha and Prakriti are absorbed in the Unmanifested; a conception which is the same as the idea underlying the Biblical expression — "remaining in the bosom of the Father".

This brings us to the doctrine of Universal Evolution as expounded by the Sages of the Wisdom-Religion.

The Spirit, or Purusha, they say, proceeds from Brahma through the various forms of matter evolved at the same time, beginning in the world of the spiritual from the highest and in the material world from the lowest form. This lowest form is one unknown as yet to modern science. Thus therefore the mineral, vegetable, and animal forms each imprison a spark of the Divine, a portion of the indivisible Purusha. These sparks struggle to "return to the Father", or in other words, to secure self-consciousness, and at last come into the highest form, on Earth, that of man, where alone self-consciousness is possible to them. The period, calculated in human time, during which this evolution goes on embraces millions of ages. Each spark of divinity has therefore millions of ages in which to accomplish its mission — that of obtaining complete self-consciousness while in the form of man. But by this is not meant that the mere act of coming into human forms of itself confers self-consciousness upon this divine spark. That great work may be accomplished during the Manvantara in which a Divine spark reaches the human form, or it may not; all depends upon the individual's own will and efforts. Each particular spirit thus goes through the Manwantara, or enters into manifestation, for its own enrichment and for that of the Whole. Mahatmas and Rishees are thus gradually evolved during a Manwantara, and become, after its expiration, planetary spirits, who guide the evolutions of other future planets. The planetary spirits of our globe are those who in previous Manwantaras — or days of Brahma — made the efforts, and became in the course of that long period Mahatmas.

Each Manwantara is for the same end and purpose, so that the Mahatmas who have now attained those heights, or those who may become such in the succeeding years of the present Manwantara, will probably be the planetary spirits of the next Manwantara for this or other planets. This system is thus seen to be based upon the identity of Spiritual Being, and, under the name of "Universal Brotherhood", constitutes the basic idea of the Theosophical Society, whose object is the realization of that Brotherhood among men.

The Sages say that this Purusha is the basis of all manifested objects. Without it nothing could exist or cohere. It interpenetrates everything everywhere. It is the reality of which, or upon which, those things called real by us are mere images. As Purusha reaches to and embraces all beings, they are all connected together; and in or on the plane where that Purusha is, there is a perfect consciousness of every act, thought, object, and circumstance, whether supposed to occur there, or on this plane, or on any other. For below the spirit and above the intellect is a plane of consciousness in which experiences are noted, commonly called man's "spiritual nature"; this is frequently said to be as susceptible of culture as his body or his intellect.

This upper plane is the real register of all sensations and experiences, although there are other registering planes. It is sometimes called "the subconscious mind". Theosophy, however, holds that it is a misuse of terms to say that the spiritual nature can be cultivated. The real object to be kept in view is to so open up or make porous the lower nature that the spiritual nature may shine through it and become the guide and ruler. It is only "cultivated" in the sense of having a vehicle prepared for its use, into which it may descend. In other words, it is held that the real man, who is the higher self — being the spark of the Divine before alluded to — overshadows the visible being, which has the possibility of becoming united to that spark. Thus it is said that the higher Spirit is not in the man, but above him.

It is always peaceful, unconcerned, blissful, and full of absolute knowledge. It continually partakes of the Divine state, being continually that state itself, "conjoined with the Gods, it feeds upon Ambrosia". The object of a student is to let the light of that spirit shine through the lower coverings.

This "spiritual culture" is only attainable as the grosser interests, passions, and demands of the flesh are subordinated to the interests, aspirations, and needs of the higher nature; and this is a matter of both system and established law.

This spirit can only become the ruler when the firm intellectual acknowledgment or admission is first made that IT alone is. And, as stated above, it being not only the person concerned but also the whole, all selfishness must be eliminated from the lower nature before its divine state can be reached. So long as the smallest personal or selfish desire — even for spiritual attainment for our own sake — remains, so long is the end desired put off. Hence the above term "demands of the flesh" really covers also demands that are not of the flesh, and its proper rendering would be "desires of the personal nature, including those of the individual soul".

When systematically trained in accordance with the aforesaid system and law, men attain to clear insight into the immaterial, spiritual world, and their interior faculties apprehend truth as immediately and readily as physical faculties grasp the things of sense, or mental faculties those of reason. Or, in the words used by some of them, "They are able to look directly upon ideas"; and hence their testimony to such truth is as trustworthy as is that of scientists or philosophers to truth in their respective fields.

In the course of this spiritual training such men acquire perception of, and control over, various forces in Nature unknown to other men, and thus are able to perform works usually called "miraculous", though really but the result of larger knowledge of natural law. What these powers are may be found in Patanjali's "Yoga Philosophy".

Their testimony as to super-sensuous truth, verified by their possession of such powers, challenges candid examination from every religious mind.

Turning now to the system expounded by these sages we find, in the first place, an account of cosmogony, the past and future of this earth and other planets, the evolution of life through elemental, mineral, vegetable, animal and human forms, as they are called.

These "passive life elementals" are unknown to modern science, though sometimes approached by it as a subtle material agent in the production of life, whereas they are a form of life itself.

Each Kalpa, or grand period, is divided into four ages or Yugas, each lasting many thousands of years, and each one being marked by a predominant characteristic. These are the Satya-yug (or age of truth), the Tretya-yug, the Dvapara-yug, and our present Kali-yug (or age of darkness), which began five thousand years back. The word "darkness" here refers to spiritual and not material darkness. In this age, however, all causes bring about their effects much more rapidly than in any other age, a fact due to the intensified momentum of "evil", as the course of its cycle is about rounding towards that of a new cycle of truth. Thus a sincere lover of the race can accomplish more in three incarnations during Kali-Yuga, than he could in a much greater number in any other age. The darkness of this age is not absolute, but is greater than that of other ages; its main tendency being towards materiality, while having some mitigation in occasional ethical or scientific advance conducive to the well-being of the race, by the removal of immediate causes of crime or disease.

Our earth is one of a chain of seven planets, it alone being on the visible plane, while the six others are on different planes, and therefore invisible. [The other planets of our solar system belong each to a chain of seven.] And the life-wave passes from the higher to the lower in the chain until it reaches our earth, and then ascends and passes to the three others on the opposite arc, and thus seven times. The evolution of forms is co-incident with this progress, the tide of life bearing with it the mineral and vegetable forms, until each globe in turn is ready to receive the human life wave. Of these globes our earth is the fourth.

Humanity passes from globe to globe in a series of Rounds, first circling about each globe, and re-incarnating upon it a fixed number of times. Concerning the human evolution on the concealed planets or globes little is permitted to be said. We have to concern ourselves with our Earth alone. The latter, when the wave of humanity has reached it for the last time (in this, our Fourth Round), began to evolute man, subdividing him into races. Each of these races when it has, through evolution, reached the period known as "the moment of choice" and decided its future destiny as an individual race, begins to disappear. The races are separated, moreover, from each other by catastrophies of nature, such as the subsidence of continents and great natural convulsions. Coincidently with the development of races the development of specialized senses takes place; thus our fifth race has so far developed five senses.

The sages further tell us that the affairs of this world and its people are subject to cyclic laws, and during any one cycle the rate or quality of progress appertaining to a different cycle is not possible. These cyclic laws operate in each age. As the ages grow darker the same laws prevail, only the cycles are shorter; that is, they are the same length in the absolute sense, but go over the given limit in a shorter period of time. These laws impose restrictions on the progress of the race. In a cycle, where all is ascending and descending, the adepts must wait until the time comes before they can aid the race to ascend. They cannot, and must not, interfere with Karmic law. Thus they begin to work actively again in the spiritual sense, when the cycle is known by them to be approaching its turning point.

At the same time these cycles have no hard lines or points of departure or inception, inasmuch as one may be ending or drawing to a close for some time after another has already begun. They thus overlap and shade into one another, as day does into night; and it is only when the one has completely ended and the other has really begun by bringing out its blossoms, that we can say we are in a new cycle. It may be illustrated by comparing two adjacent cycles to two interlaced circles, where the circumference of one touches the centre of the other, so that the moment where one ended and the other began would be at the point where the circumferences intersected each other. Or by imagining a man as representing, in the act of walking, the progress of the cycles; his rate of advancement can only be obtained by taking the distance covered by his paces, the points at the middle of each pace, between the feet, being the beginning of cycles and their ending.

The cyclic progress is assisted, or the deterioration further permitted, in this way; at a time when the cycle is ascending, developed and progressed Beings, known in Sanscrit by the term *Gnanis*, descend to this earth from other spheres where the cycle is going down, in order that they may also help the spiritual progress of this globe. In like manner they leave this sphere when our cycle approaches darkness. These *Gnanis* must not, however, be confounded with the Mahatmas and Adepts mentioned above. The right aim of true theosophists should therefore be so to live that their influence may be conducive for the dispelling of darkness to the end that such Gnanis may turn again towards this sphere.

Theosophy also teaches the existence of a universally diffused and highly ethereal medium, which has been called the "Astral Light" and "Akâsa". It is the repository of all past, present, and future events, and in it are recorded the effects of spiritual causes, and of all acts and thoughts from the direction of either spirit or matter. It may be called the Book of the Recording Angel.

Akâsa, however, is a misnomer when it is confused with Ether or the Astral light of the Kabalists. Akâsa is the noumenon of the phenomenal Ether or Astral light proper, for Akâsa is infinite, impartite, intangible, its only procuction being Sound. [Akâsa in the mysticism of the esoteric philosophy is properly speaking the female "Holy Ghost"; "Sound" or speech being the logos, the manifested verbum of the unmanifested Mother. See Sankhyasara Preface p 33 *et seq.*]

And this Astral light is material and not spirit. It is, in fact, the lower principle of that cosmic body of which Akâsa is the highest. It has the power of retaining all images. This includes a statement that each thought as well as word and act makes an image there. These images may be said to have two lives, 1st. Their own as an image. 2nd. The impress left by them in the matrix of the astral light. In the upper realm of this light there is no such thing as space or time in the human sense. All future events are the thoughts and acts of men; these are producers in advance of the picture of the event which is to occur. Ordinary men continually, recklessly, and wickedly, are making these events sure to come to pass, but the Sages, Mahatmas, and the Adepts of the good law, make only such pictures as are in accordance with Divine law, because they control the production of their thought. In the Astral light are all the differentiated sounds as well. The elementals are energic centres in it. The shades of departed human beings and animals are also there. Hence, any seer or entranced person can see in it all that anyone had done or said, as well as that which had happened to anyone with whom he is connected. Hence, also, the identity of deceased persons — who are supposed to report specially out of this plane — is not to be concluded from the giving of forgotten or unknown words, facts, or ideas. Out of this plane of matter can be taken the pictures of all who have ever lived, and then reflected on a suitable magneto-electrical surface, so as to seem like the apparition of the deceased, producing all the sensations of weight, hardness, and extension.

Through the means of the Astral Light and the help of Elementals, the various material elements may be drawn down and precipitated from the atmosphere upon either a plane surface or in the form of a solid object; this precipitation may be made permanent, or it may be of such a light cohesive power as to soon fade away. But the help of the elementals can only be obtained by a strong will added to a complete knowledge of the laws which govern the being of the elementals. It is useless to give further details on this point; first, because the untrained student cannot understand; and second, the complete explanation is not permitted, were it even possible in this space.

The world of the elementals is an important factor in our world and in the course of the student. Each thought as it is evolved by a man coalesces instantly with an Elemental, and is then beyond the man's power.

It can easily be seen that this process is going on every instant. Therefore each thought exists as a entity. Its length of life depends on two things: (a) The original force of the person's will and thought; (b) The power of the elemental which coalesced with it, the latter being determined by the class to which the elemental belongs. This is the case with good and bad thoughts alike, and as the will beneath the generality of wicked thoughts is usually powerful, we can see that the result is very important, because the elemental has no conscience and obtains its constitution and direction from the thought it may from time to time carry.

Each human being has his own elementals that partake of his nature and his thoughts. If you fix your thoughts upon a person in anger, or in critical, uncharitable judgment, you attract to yourself a number of those elementals that belong to, generate, and are generated by this particular fault or failing, and they precipitate themselves upon you. Hence, through the injustice of your merely human condemnation, which cannot know the source and causes of the action of another, you at once become a sharer of his fault or failing by your own act, and the spirit expelled returns "with seven devils worse than himself". This is the origin of the popular saying that "curses, like chickens, come home to roost", and has its root in the laws governing magnetic affinity.

In the Kali-Yuga we are hypnotized by the effect of the immense body of images in the Astral Light, compounded of all the deeds, thoughts, and so forth of our ancestors, whose lives tended in a material direction. These images influence the inner man — who is conscious of them — by suggestion. In a brighter age the influence of such images would be towards Truth. The effect of the Astral Light, as thus moulded and painted by us, will remain so long as we continue to place those images there, and it thus becomes our judge and our executioner. Every universal law thus contains within itself the means for its own accomplishment and the punishment for its violation, and requires no further authority to postulate it or to carry out its decrees.

The Astral Light by its inherent action both evolves and destroys forms. It is the universal register. Its chief office is that of a vehicle for the operation of the laws of Karma, or the progress of the principle of life, and it is thus in a deep spiritual sense a medium or "mediator" between man and his Deity — his higher spirit.

Theosophy also tells of the origin, history, development, and destiny of mankind.

Upon the subject of Man it teaches:—

1. That each spirit is a manifestation of the One Spirit, and thus a part of all. It passes through a series of experiences in incarnation, and is destined to ultimate reunion with the Divine.

2. That this incarnation is not single but repeated, each individuality becoming re-embodied during numerous existences in successive races and planets of our chain, and accumulating the experiences of each incarnation towards its perfection.

3. That between adjacent incarnations, after grosser elements are first purged away, comes a period of comparative rest and refreshment, called Devachan, the soul being therein prepared for its next advent into material life.

The constitution of man is subdivided in a septenary manner, the main divisions being those of body, soul and spirit. These divisions and their relative development govern his subjective condition after death. The real division cannot be understood, and must for a time remain esoteric, because it requires certain senses not usually developed for its understanding. If the present sevenfold division, as given by Theosophical writers, is adhered to strictly and without any conditional statement, it will give rise to controversy or error. For instance, Spirit is not a seventh principle. It is the synthesis, or the whole, and is equally present in the other six. The present various divisions can only be used as a general working hypothesis, to be developed and corrected as students advance and themselves develop.

The state of spiritual but comparative rest known as Devachan is not an eternal one, and so is not the same as the eternal heaven of Christianity. Nor does "hell" correspond to the state known to theosophical writers as Avitchi.

All such painful states are transitory and purificatory states. When those are passed the individual goes into Devachan.

"Hell" and Avitchi are thus not the same. Avitchi is the same as the "second death", as it is in fact annihilation that only comes to the "black Magician" or spiritually wicked, as will be seen further on.

The nature of each incarnation depends upon the balance as struck of the merit and demerit of the previous life or lives — upon the way in which the man has lived and thought; and this law is inflexible and wholly just.

"Karma" — a term signifying two things, the law of ethical causation (Whatsoever a man soweth, that shall he also reap); and the balance or excess of merit or demerit in any individual, determines also the main experiences of joy and sorrow in each incarnation, so that what we call "luck" is in reality "desert" — desert acquired in past existence.

Karma is not all exhausted in a single life, nor is a person necessarily in this life experiencing the effect of all his previous Karma; for some may be held back by various causes. The principal cause is the failure of the Ego to acquire a body which will furnish the instrument or apparatus in and by which the meditation or thoughts of previous lives can have their effect and be ripened. Hence it is held that there is a mysterious power in the man's thoughts during a life, sure to bring about its results in either an immediately succeeding life or in one many lives distant; that is, in whatever life the Ego obtains a body capable of being the focus, apparatus, or instrument for the ripening of past Karma. There is also a swaying or diverging power in Karma in its effect upon the soul, for a certain course of life — or thought — will influence the soul in that direction for sometimes three lives, before the beneficial, or bad, effect of any other sort of Karma must be felt. Nor does it follow that every minute portion of Karma must be felt in the same detail as when produced, for several sorts of Karma may come to a head together at one point in the life, and, by their combined effect, produce a result which, while, as a whole, accurately representing all the elements in it, still is a different Karma from each single component part. This may be known as the nullification of the postulated effect of the classes of Karma involved.

The process of evolution up to re-union with the Divine is and includes successive elevations from rank to rank of power and usefulness. The most exalted beings still in the flesh are known as Sages, Rishees, Brothers, Masters. Their great function being the preservation at all times, and when cyclic laws permit, the extension, of spiritual knowledge and influence.

When union with the Divine is effected, all the events and experiences of each incarnation are known.

As to the process of spiritual development, Theosophy teaches: —

1. That the essence of the process lies in the securing of supremacy, to the highest, the spiritual, element of man's nature.
2. That this is attained along four lines, among others, —
(a) The entire eradication of selfishness in all forms, and the cultivation of *broad, generous* sympathy in, and effort for the good of others.
(b) The absolute cultivation of the inner, spiritual man by meditation, by reaching to and communion with the Divine, and by exercise of the kind described by Patanjali, *i.e.*, incessant striving to an ideal end.
(c) The control of fleshly appetites and desires, all lower, material interests being deliberately subordinated to the behests of the spirits.
(d) The careful performance of every duty belonging to one's station in life, without desire for reward, leaving results for Divine law.
3. That while the above is incumbent on and practicable by all religiously disposed men, a yet higher plane of spiritual attainment is conditioned upon a specific course of training, physical, intellectual, and spiritual, by which the internal faculties are first aroused and then developed.
4. That an extension of this process is reached in Adeptship, Mahatma-ship, or the states of Rishees, Sages, and Dhyan Chohans, which are all exalted stages, attained by laborious self-discipline and hardship, protracted through possibly many incarnations, and with many degrees of initiation and preferment, beyond which are yet other stages ever approaching the Divine.

As to the rationale of spiritual development it asserts: —

1. That the process takes place entirely within the individual himself, the motive, the effort, and the result proceeding from his own inner nature, along the lines of self-evolution.

2. That, however personal and interior, this process is not unaided, being possible, in fact, only through close communion with the supreme source of all strength.

As to the degree of advancement in incarnations it holds:

1. That even a mere intellectual acquaintance with Theosophic truth has great value in fitting the individual for a step upwards in his next earth-life, as it gives an impulse in that direction.

2. That still more is gained by a career of duty, piety, and beneficence,

3. That a still greater advance is attained by the attentive and devoted use of the means to spiritual culture heretofore stated.

4. That every race and individual of it reaches in evolution a period known as "the moment of choice", when they decide for themselves their future destiny by a deliberate and conscious choice between eternal life and death, and that this right of choice is the peculiar appanage of the free soul. It cannot be exercised until the man has realized the soul within him, and until that soul has attained some measure of self-consciousness in the body. The moment of choice is not a fixed period of time; it is made up of all moments. It cannot come unless all the previous lives have led up to it. For the race as a whole it has not yet come. Any individual can hasten the advent of this period for himself under the previously stated law of the ripening of Karma, Should he then fail to choose right he is not wholly condemned, for the economy of nature provides that he shall again and again have the opportunity of choice when the moment arrives for the whole race. After this period the race, having blossomed, tends towards its dissolution. A few individuals of it will have outstripped its progress and attained Adeptship or Mahatmaship. The main body, who have chosen aright, but who have not attained salvation, pass into the subjective condition, there to await the influx of the human life wave into the next globe, which they are the first souls to people, the deliberate choosers of evil, whose lives are passed in great spiritual wickedness (for

evil done for the sheer love of evil *per se*), sever the connection with the Divine Spirit, or the monad, which for ever abandons the human Ego. Such Egos pass into the misery of the eighth sphere, as far as we understand, there to remain until the separation between what they had thus cultivated and the personal Ishwar or divine spark is complete. But this tenet has never been explained to us by the Masters, who have always refused to answer and to explain it conclusively. At the next Manwantara that Divine Spark will probably begin again the long evolutionary journey, being cast into the stream of life at the source and passing upward again through all the lower forms.

So long as the connection with the Divine Monad is not severed, this annihilation of personality cannot take place. Something of that personality will always remain attached to the immortal Ego. Even after such severance the human being may live on, a man among men — a soul-less being. This disappointment, so to call it, of the Divine Spark by depriving it of its chosen vehicle constitutes the "sin against the Holy Ghost", which its very nature forbade it to pardon, because it cannot continue an association with principles which have become degraded and vitiated in the absolute sense, so that they no longer respond to cyclic or evolutionary impulses, but, weighted by their own nature, sink to the lowest depths of matter. The connection, once wholly broken, cannot in the nature of Being be resumed. But innumerable opportunities for return offer themselves throughout the dissolving process, which lasts thousands of years.

There is also a fate that comes to even adepts of the Good Law which is somewhat similar to a loss of "heaven" after the enjoyment for incalculable periods of time. When the adept has reached a certain very high point in his evolution he may, by a mere wish, become what the Hindus call, a "Deva" — or lesser god. If he does this, then, although he will enjoy the bliss and power of that state for a vast length of time, he will not at the next Pralaya partake of the conscious life "in the bosom of the Father", but has to pass down into matter at the next new "creation", performing certain functions that could not be now made clear, and has to come up again through the elemental world; but this fate is not like that of the Black Magician who falls into Avitchi. And again between the two he can choose the middle state and become a Nirmanakaya — one who gives up the Bliss of Nirvana and remains in conscious existence outside of his body after its death: in order to help Humanity. This is the greatest sacrifice he can do for mankind. By advancement from one degree of interest and comparative attainment to another as above stated, the student hastens the advent of the moment of choice, after which his rate of progress is greatly intensified.

It may be added that Theosophy is the only system of religion and philosophy which gives satisfactory explanation of such problems as these: —

1. The object, use, and inhabitation of other planets than this earth, which planets serve to complete and to prolong the evolutionary course, and to fill the required measure of the universal experience of souls.

2. The geological cataclysms of earth; the frequent absence of intermediate types in its fauna; the occurrence of architectural and other relics of races now lost, and as to which ordinary science has nothing but vain conjecture; the nature of extinct civilizations and the causes of their extinction; the persistence of savagery and the unequal development of existing civilization; the differences, physical and internal, between the various races of men; the line of future development.

3. The contrasts and unisons of the world's faiths, and the common foundation underlying them all.

4. The existence of evil, of suffering; and of sorrow, — a hopeless puzzle to the mere philanthropist or theologian.

5. The inequalities in social condition and privilege; the sharp contrasts between wealth and poverty, intelligence and stupidity, culture and ignorance, virtue and vileness; the appearance of men of genius in families destitute of it, as well as other facts in conflict with the law of heredity; the frequent cases of unfitness of environment around individuals, so sore as to embitter disposition, hamper aspiration, and paralyse endeavour; the violent antithesis between character and

condition; the occurrence of accident, misfortune, and untimely death; — all of them problems solvable only by either the conventional theory of Divine caprice or the Theosophic doctrines of Karma and Re-incarnation.

6. The possession by individuals of psychic powers — clairvoyance, clairaudience, etc., as well as the phenomena of psychometry and statuvolism.

7. The true nature of genuine phenomena in spiritualism, and the proper antidote to superstition and to exaggerated expectation.

8. The failure of conventional religions to greatly extend their areas, reform abuses, re-organize society, expand the idea of brotherhood, abate discontent, diminish crime, and elevate humanity; and an apparent inadequacy to realize in individual lives the ideal they professedly uphold.

The above is a sketch of the main features of Theosophy, the Wisdom-Religion. Its details are to be found in the rapidly-growing literature upon the subject.

There are three stages of interest, developed by the study of Theosophy:

1. That of intellectual inquiry, — to be met by works in Public Libraries, etc..

2. That of desire for personal culture, — to be met partly by the books prepared for that specific end, partly by the periodical Magazines expounding Theosophy.

3. That of personal identification with the Theosophical Society, an association formed in 1875 with three aims, — to be the nucleus of a Universal Brotherhood; to promote the study of Aryan and other Eastern literatures, religions, and sciences; to investigate unexplained laws of nature and the psychical powers latent in man. Adhesion to the first only is a pre-requisite to membership, the others being optional. The Society represents no particular creed, is entirely unsectarian, and includes professors of all faiths, only exacting from each member that toleration of the beliefs of others which he desires them to exhibit towards his own.

WHAT ARE THEOSOPHISTS ?

With how much of the Nature-searching, God-seeking science of the ancient Aryan and Greek mystics, and of the powers of modern spiritual mediumship, does the Theosophical Society agree ? Our answer is: — With it all. But if asked what it believes in, the reply will be: — "As a body — Nothing". The society, as a body, has no creed, for creeds are but the shells of unspiritual knowledge; and Theosophy in its fruition is spiritual knowledge itself — the very essence of philosophical and theistic enquiry. Visible representative of Universal Theosophy, it can be no more sectarian than a Geographical Society, which represents universal geographic exploration without caring whether the explorers be of one creed or another. The religion of the Society is an algebraical equation, in which, so long as the sign of equality is not omitted, each member is free to substitute quantities of his own, which accord better with climatic and other exigencies of his native land, with the idiosyncrasies of his people, or even with his own. Having no accepted creed, our Society is very ready to give and take, to learn and teach, by practical experimentation, as opposed to mere passive and credulous acceptance of enforced dogma. It is willing to accept every result claimed by any school or system that can be logically and experimentally demonstrated. Conversely, it can take nothing on mere faith, no matter by whom the demand may be made.....

Born in the United States of America, the Society was constituted on the model of its Mother-land. The latter, omitting the name of God from its constitution, lest it should one day afford a pretext to make a State religion, gives absolute equality to all religions in its laws. All support and each is in turn protected by the State. The Society modelled upon this constitution may fairly be termed "a republic of Conscience".

Our members, as individuals, are free to stay outside or inside any creed they please, provided they do not pretend that none but themselves shall enjoy the privilege of conscience, and try to force their opinions upon the others. The Theosophical Society tries to act upon the wisdom of the old Buddhistic axiom: — "Honour thine own faith, and do not slander that of others" ....

Broader and far more universal in its views than any existing mere scientific Society, it has, plus science, its belief in every possibility and the determined will to penetrate into those unknown spiritual regions which exact science proclaims that its votaries have no business to explore. And it has one quality more than any religion in that it makes no difference between Gentile, Jew or Christian. It is in this spirit that the Society has been established upon the footing of a Universal Brotherhood.

THEOSOPHICAL CONCEPTS OF EVOLUTION AND RELIGION

THERE is a close connection between Evolution and Religion, because Religion is a manifestation of those evolutionary tendencies which are leading mankind, through cycle after cycle, towards that spirituality and perfection of being which we now conceive of and express under the term *God*.

Evolution in its widest signification implies the development, unfolding, or growth of the perceptive faculties or functions, so as to enlarge the consciousness in relation to its environments. In other words, it is the gradual extension of the boundaries of consciousness. It is the expansion of that internal and hidden principle of life which pervades all nature, and which manifests itself on the outward or material plane in an endless variety of progressive forms, from that which we term *dead* matter up to the highly organized, complex, and self-conscious structure of the human body.

Evolution is that universal principle which forbids anything to stand still. There exists in all things a perpetual inherent strain or tendency towards something which is dimly perceived to be possible in the future. That which exists in the concrete must first exist in the abstract. The real is the sequence of the ideal. There must be a possibility for the ideal, otherwise it could not exist. We see this in every department of human activity. The man of genius is he who grasps the ideal with so firm a hold that he can bring it down in some concrete form to the perception of his fellow-men. The ideal is always pressing in upon us. As human beings, we are conscious of the strain in a great variety of ways. On the plane of the senses it exists as *desire*, and leads men on in restless activity, which is never satisfied even in the attainment of its object; for nothing is more characteristic of human ambition than that the moment the goal is actually reached, or the cup of pleasure raised to the lips, the object appears worthless, there is still a further goal to reach, or the cup of pleasure becomes a draught of poison.

Men are driven at last, by reason of the universality of this experience, into fixing their desires and hopes on a higher plane, where they imagine that the obstacles to their enjoyment of that happiness which they are ever seeking but never finding, will cease to exist; and they turn instinctively to religion for guidance and comfort. But the religious instinct is not merely born of repeated failures to obtain happiness on the material plane. It exists as a *strain* or evolutionary tendency of the higher or spiritual part of our nature, which has its own laws of progression corresponding to those which operate on the physical plane. It is indeed, more strictly speaking, the operation of this *strain* on the higher planes which causes that progression of more and more highly organized forms in the physical world, which is what Science understands by the term Evolution. *Occult* science traces the evolutionary wave through three elemental kingdoms of nature, from thence through the mineral, vegetable, and animal, in succession, until it reaches the human. That which really evolves, the individual *monad*, assumes, time after time, a fresh form or personality, and requires, as the result of its growing consciousness, a more and more perfect organization in which to function. We do not perceive the real man, the Ego, because he exists on a higher plane than that of the physical senses, but we have some conception of this higher principle in that which we term *character*, and we may read the signature of the real man in the structure of the various parts of the body, the formation of the head, the physiognomy, the shape and lines of the hand, etc. A man who has no generosity, for instance, in his character, will be deficient in certain physical developments which correspond to this quality of the soul. Nature works on clear and definite lines, and similar forces at work on the higher planes will produce similar manifestations on the lower. In this way we come to a knowledge of the higher through the lower, in which we see the higher reflected. So long as our consciousness is centred on the lower, we take the reflection for the real. This is what science is doing at the present day. Science deals with the laws which operate on the material plane, and with regard to the law of evolution she has been able to trace a certain progression of species, and more than suspects, though she cannot actually prove, that the higher forms of life have developed in turn through all the lower; but of those higher and subtle forces in nature by reason of which this progression takes places, she knows absolutely nothing.

Science is agnostic in reference to anything that transcends the material plane, and regards consciousness as inherent in our physiological functions, it being the evolution of these functions which brings an increase of consciousness, and this consciousness has reached the highest perfection in man because he has the most highly organized body, and more particularly the best developed brain. This view docs not permit of any previous existence for that consciousness which is now centred in any particular human being, neither does it permit of any existence for it outside of the physical organization, or after the death of the same; unless indeed, we conceive in some sort of way of a spiritual body being hatched out of the physical.

Science may appear superficially to be leading men into Agnosticism and Atheism, but this is only a passing phase. The value of the scientific work of the age is to be found in those broad generalizations and conceptions of the working of natural law, which finds one principle acting alike in both great and small; and when men have grasped firmly the unity, harmony, and solidarity of the physical universe, they have only to carry their conceptions one step forward, to assimilate their knowledge with their intuition, to carry their conceptions of natural law into the spiritual world, to grasp firmly the universal principle of *Love*, and they will find themselves in possession of a religion founded on reason and knowledge; they will find that science has led them up to a far grander *Monotheism* than that which it was the supposed special mission of the Jewish race to proclaim, and of the Messias to complete.

In the meanwhile it would appear inevitable that in the reaction from the intellectual and moral bondage of priestcraft and dogma, men should turn to science for that infallibility which they ever desire, and should lose sight for the time being of the possibilities of their spiritual ideal, in those scientific discoveries and inventions which have revolutionized the conditions of civilization in the present century. There is a danger lest materialism should swallow up all spiritual insight, and men become still further immersed in the illusions of the senses. The individual may pass through this stage in the natural development of his conceptions, and the experience of the individual is repeated on a larger scale in the community, the nation, and the race. But the spiritual forces at work in a man will not allow him to maintain this position long. Sooner or later he must come face to face with his higher self, of whose existence he has hitherto been only dimly conscious. In the far back ages of human history we find that this consciousness took the form of the grossest superstition and idolatry, such as we find prevailing in some races at the present day; but as the Ego accumulates experience in a sequence of lives or incarnations on the physical plane, he is gradually lifted out of superstition by the aid of reason and knowledge, and there comes a time when he has to bring his intellectual faculties to bear upon those religious dogmas which he has hitherto accepted as authoritative and infallible.

If a man is a religionist merely on account of feeling, sentiment, emotion, or fear which he cannot analyse or define, he will belong to that religion which prevails in the community into which he is born; he will be a slave to the religious opinions of the time, and unable to free himself from the bondage of orthodoxy, from the accumulated mass of formula and dogma which overlies the universal truth.

The intellectual phase of the evolutionary process is largely operative in the present age, and is leading men, in the reaction from superstition, into an attempt to determine all questions by the aid of the intellect alone. The present generation is engaged in intellectually examining the credentials of religion; and religion, as represented by the church, has by no means a liking for the process.

Dogmatic religion is not reasonable; it distinctly repudiates the reasoning faculties, and refuses to permit the intellect to exercise its function of discrimination. To the Christian of today there is no appeal beyond the Bible, and what he conceives to be the interpretation thereof. The Mahomedan equally swears by his Koran, and so with the sacred books of every other religion. When the time comes, however, in a man's experience for his creed to be confronted by his reason, he finds that those doctrines which he has hitherto regarded as sacred and infallible, are not so regarded by others, and that the authority of his own particular church is only one of a great number of conflicting authorities. This is a sad blow to his faith, and he then endeavours to find some intellectual basis, some unanswerable argument in support of his cherished belief. Many men succeed in doing this, or succeed just up to that point where it is most desirable that knowledge and reason should take the place of authority and dogma. Beyond this point they affirm that it is impossible to go, and that what remains is a matter of divine revelation, and can only be grasped — so far as our present life is concerned — by means of *faith*. On the other hand, a man's *faith* may utterly break down in the effort to discriminate between one belief and another, and as often as not he is driven into atheism and an unreasoning contempt for all religion whatsoever.

Man's experience works in cycles, and after rising to the spiritual plane through the emotions of religion, he may again descend into matter, and working through the intellectual plane, he will re-ascend to the spiritual, *plus knowledge*. While on the descending arc he loses sight of the spiritual part of his nature, but on the ascending arc this grows brighter and clearer, and becomes self-conscious, as the result of the experience through which the Ego has passed. There are many such cycles in the evolution of the Ego, the real man, and what is true of the individual is true of the race and also of the whole universe. There is only one law operating in both great and small. That which takes place in the individual unit is a reflection of similar processes which are repeated in ever-increasing magnitudes throughout the circle of eternity. The microcosm reflects the macrocosm. As above so below, is the fundamental truth by which we are able to transfer our knowledge to that which is unseen, and grasp those universal principles which must become the basis of our *faith*. There is a law of correspondences which enables us to penetrate deeper and still deeper into the workings of nature, but we shall never find a break, we shall never find a *spiritual* world where there is no *natural* law, nor a natural world where spirit is not ever present. The triangles are interlaced. Night and day, summer and winter, these are smaller cycles within the larger ones to which they correspond, and which stretch out in an endless succession of Kalpas and Yugas; the days and nights of Brahmâ; the Manvantaras and the Pralayas. The activity of the day is followed by the unconsciousness and sleep of night. So is our life. The sleep of death is followed by a reawakening, and the man takes up his real life-task at the point at which he left off. As the actions of yesterday are related to those of today, so are those of our previous incarnation related to the present one, and the present becomes the potentiality of the future.

Occult Science possesses an accurate knowledge of the duration of those cycles through which the human race has to pass in its evolution as a whole, from the lower forms of matter up to that unity with the Divine principle which is its ultimate goal.

In the meantime, with regard to that personality in the physical plane which is all that most people know of *man*, this personality may be the expression of any of the many stages in the evolutionary process. The race, as a whole, progresses, because the individual units progress, but the individual units do not keep pace with each other, for in that case there could be no difference of opinion in the world; for all would be in exactly the same state of consciousness, and would perceive things in the same light. The present personality of the man, therefore, represents merely a passing phase in the history of the real man, in the descent of the spirit into matter, and its reascent to the spiritual-plane *plus* self-consciousness. The real man, the Ego, the Divine Ray, must incarnate, must see itself reflected in matter in order to attain to self-consciousness, just as the individual must see his personality reflected in a glass so long as he is unable to step outside of that personality in order to view it.

Until the man has attained to spiritual self-consciousness he will be unable to recognize the illusory and transient nature of that reflection which forms his present personality, and will regard the personality as a real thing, having a separate and isolated existence. Not until the spirit has become fully self-conscious will its evolution on this plane be complete, and the necessity for reincarnation cease to exist. On the physical plane everything is subject to the law of change, there is no permanent state.

The personality cannot endure. It fades away with the exhaustion of those forces which produced it, and the spirit sinks into the sleep of death, to reawaken with a new personality, the conditions of which have been determined by the "Karma" of its past incarnation.

In various parts of the world, in different nations and races, we find men in every stage of the evolutionary process, from the savage to the philosopher, and still higher. You cannot make a Plato or a Newton, a Christ or a Buddha, out of a Fetish worshipper in his present incarnation, but you must grant him the possibility of becoming one in a future age; and meanwhile he finds an expression or reflection of that state of consciousness at which he has arrived in one or other of those concrete forms of superstition or religion in which the universal truth finds a partial expression.

Like the movement of a so-called *fixed* star, so is the evolution of a unit of the human race. A thousand years are scarcely sufficient to determine that it does actually move, and our present conceptions of time and space are utterly inadequate to deal with those magnitudes with which we stand face to face, and which we name eternity. It is well that it is so. It is well that we cannot remember the processes by which we have reached our present stage, nor form an adequate conception of that which awaits us. It is well that the sleep of death should obliterate all memory of our previous incarnation, leaving only the aroma, the essence, as a permanent addition to the character of our real, our higher self. To most people one short life-time appears all too long, too hard, too much fraught with sorrow and suffering to be worth living save for the reward of an eternity of bliss. It is well that religion should speak of Heaven to sustain those whose faith is weak, and it is well that she should hold the terrors of Hell over those who cannot perceive the inherent quality of evil. The personality of man shrinks to naught before the infinity of time and space, but in his essence he is Divine, and if he would rise to a knowledge of his divinity and claim his birthright as a "Son of God", he must learn to live in the Eternal, to participate in that consciousness which knows neither time nor space. The illusions of matter must cease to throw a veil over his spiritual perceptions, and human hopes, fears, and passions no longer subjugate him, and bring his spirit back to earth on the current of unsatisfied desire.

To unite religion and science, spiritual truth and natural law, that is what men require in the present age; and having need of this larger knowledge they shall surely find it. Science is slowly leading men up to that conception of the unity of nature which will enable them ultimately to free themselves altogether from the bondage of superstition, and grasp that universal principle which finds its expression in each and every religion. And when men are prepared for this larger knowledge it will take possession of them and become the spirit of the age; for there are those who, having gone before, have become masters and adepts in the higher wisdom, and are ever ready to impart their knowledge to those who are spiritually prepared to receive it.

It is because the age is to some extent ripe for the reception of this larger knowledge that a portion of it has lately been given to the world through the medium of the Theosophical Society and its founders. This knowledge constitutes a portion of the ancient Wisdom Religion, or Secret Doctrine, which was never given to the masses in its esoteric form, but which is the basis of every exoteric religion, and is taught in the Bible as in every other sacred book in every nation and tongue. It is purposely wrapped up in allegory and fable, the lives of historical personages being often taken as the narrative basis. The Church cannot interpret the Bible, for she has lost the key, and clings blindly and doggedly to the letter that killeth, while the spirit of knowledge which men seek has to be found elsewhere. Men turn from the narrow conceptions of the Church to that light which science offers. Ofttimes the reaction leads them to accept the dogma of science with as much unreason as they previously showed in clinging to the dogma of religion; but a basis will surely be found which will make religion scientific and science religious. Such a basis is that which Theosophy now offers to the world, and it remains to be seen how far that which Theosophy teaches can meet the wants of the race in its present stage of evolution.

There exists a great tendency, in reference to Theosophical teachings, to regard these as being merely a set of doctrines which are to take the place of existing forms of religion. It is, perhaps, inevitable that this should be so, owing to the limited ideas of the majority of men in reference to the scope, claims, and authority of religion, in the common acceptation of the term, and the persistency with which the human mind clings to *form*, to that which is material and tangible. The result of this is, that Theosophy is looked upon in the light of a competitor by those who wield the power of authority in the various churches and sects, and that even those who are sufficiently impartial to give the subject any consideration, do so in the hope of finding some authoritative doctrines which shall take the place of certain others, respecting which they may have their doubts.

Strictly speaking, Theosophy does not teach any doctrine whatever, but there are certain primary concepts which belong essentially to Theosophy, and without which it could not become the common platform on which men of every race and creed can unite. Theosophy looks upon the human race as a whole; its creed is the Brotherhood of Humanity, and its practice Altruism. A Theosophist may be a Christian or a Jew, a Mahomedan or a Buddhist, or any other shade of opinion whatever in the matter of religion, from various causes connected with that progressive state of his real ego, which we have already sketched out; but he can claim no monopoly of truth, and must grant to his fellow-men an equal right to those opinions and beliefs which they may hold for the time being. That such an universal spirit of toleration may prevail is proved by the success which has attended the efforts of the Theosophical Society, and by the thousands of all shades of opinion who have openly joined the movement. But still the power of authority holds sway over the majority of human minds, and the *orthodox* of every religion will still continue to regard all other religions, and Theosophy in particular, as a delusion and a snare.

Take, for instance, the Christian, religion, with which perhaps the majority of our readers are more familiar than with any other. What does *orthodox* Christianity teach to those who are brought up within its influence? It teaches first and fundamentally that it alone is the one truth concerning God and his dealings with man; that to be outside the Christian Church is to be outside the divine favour; that those who reject the Christian teachings are lost sinners, and that the millions who never heard of Christ, are heathens who must perish under the curse of Adam, unless the teachings of the Bible can be brought to them in time. Now let us consider that in this belief millions of men and women have been brought up without any means of knowing better, and that millions of children are being educated in the same manner. We all know how strong is the effect of early training, and how it clings to a man all through his life, however much he may appear to have broken loose from its restraints. When a man who has lived a careless and worldly life finds himself at last on the brink of the grave, his mind reverts to what little he learnt of religion in his early days, and as a drowning man catches at a straw so will he endeavour to obtain some hope to which he can look in the darkness that is closing round him.

It requires a strong individuality, and a wide view of humanity, to enable a man to lift himself out of the bondage of custom and habit. The narrowness and provincialism of the man who has never left his country village is a standing proverb. He judges everything by the standard that pertains to his own little circle of neighbours and acquaintances. Of the great world outside he may know something by report, but he can have only a very inadequate conception of any state of society other than that in which he lives; and should he chance to go out into the greater world, his provincialism is patent in all his doings and sayings. The man who lives only in one narrow religious circle is just as absurd, just as provincial in his ideas as the countryman who knows nothing of the larger life of the city, where the forces which mould the destinies of the nation are centred, and intensified a thousand-fold, and beat and surge in great waves of human passion and suffering. It is the faculty of living in the larger life of humanity, of grasping the principles which underlie the phenomena, which distinguishes the poet and the artist, the statesman, philosopher, and man of science.

It is only by getting *outside* of a thing that we can view that thing in its due proportion, and assign to it its proper place in relation to the whole. The more we enlarge our consciousness, the smaller becomes the importance of those objects in which it was previously centred. We need to rise above the influence of human passions, hopes, and fears, before we can view these in their proper light. The man who lives in his religion as the countryman lives in his village, and refuses to believe that there is any comfort or safety outside of it, fails to grasp that larger conception of humanity which is the first principle of Theosophy. He fails to grasp the principles which underlie the phenomena, and which make one man a Christian and another a Buddhist, and all equal in the sight of God.

If we say that this is what every *orthodox* religionist does, we shall say that no *orthodox* person can be a *Theosophist*, though he may be member of the Theosophical Society. Of course there are all grades and shades of orthodoxy: "orthodoxy is my doxy, heterodoxy is your doxy", said Dr. Johnson. But inasmuch as orthodoxy is exclusive, it cannot recognise the fundamental concept of Theosophy, which makes no distinction between orthodoxy and heterodoxy. You cannot have an orthodox Theosophist, because a man is either a Theosophist or he is not one; he has either stepped outside the line which orthodoxy draws between one belief and another, or else he remains within his own narrow creed.

It is undoubtedly a fact that within the Christian Church there is now a much broader and more enlightened spirit than could have been supposed to exist some fifty or even twenty-five years ago, but if the church gives way once she may give way again. If she abandons doctrines which were previously held to be the very essence and essential of religion, where is the final point, the ground from which she cannot be driven?

With the progress of knowledge, civilization, and science, the conflict which is ever being waged between the new and the old, between established conceptions, hereditary faith, creeds, dogmas, and doctrines — owing much of their power and influence to the very fact of their being established and in possession of the field — is ever changing its ground. Some new generalization, deeper and more comprehensive than any which have preceded it, claims the attention of the conflicting parties, and is raised as a banner round which the fight concentrates. It is most difficult to uproot established ideas of whatever kind, whether in our own mind or that of the community. An established cause has not merely its votaries but its vested interests, it has not merely those who uphold it through force of habit, hereditary conviction, or social convenience, but it has its institutions, its priesthood, and a host of those who are vitally interested, either directly or indirectly, in its maintenance. Hence it arises that any innovation which threatens to overturn the existing order is met by deadly hatred. This is not merely the case as between religion and science. It is exemplified in history in a thousand ways, and we cannot expect that religious institutions should be exempt from the general law. Not merely, however, is religion, not exempt, but it is the most striking example that can be found. Religion, dealing as it does with man's highest nature, with his most powerful instincts, appealing to his inmost heart and conscience, and professing to be his guide and mentor in this world, and his hope of salvation in the next, exercises such a sway over his mind and imagination that an institution such as the Church is far more powerful than any merely secular organization; nor have there ever been wanting men who seized upon this enormous power, and wielded it for their own ambitious purposes. At the time when the church exercised a temporal as well as a spiritual power, she used that power with terrible effect, and wrote upon the page of history a blackened record of fire and blood. The Church of the present day professes to look with abhorrence on the past history of priestcraft, but the spirit of intolerance and persecution still exists, and there are not wanting in the present time examples of terrorism and cruelty exercised in the name of religion.

History presents to us several well-defined points or centres round which the conflict between science and religion has raged at different times, and in which religion has always been worsted. Such, for instance, was the controversy respecting the position of the earth in relation to the solar system, in which Galileo led the way on the part of science. This was the conflict between the Church and astronomy, in which science has been finally and conclusively victorious. Next we have the conflict with geology, and the controversy respecting the age of the earth, in which matter the church still clings to the Mosaic records. Then followed the grand generalization of science contained in the doctrine of the conservation of energy, which struck at the very root of what religion conceived to be necessary for the exercise of the creative and administrative power of a personal God. In the present day it is evolution which appears as a monster, threatening to swallow up all that religion can still cling to in Biblical cosmogony. Evolution strikes at one of the oldest and most deeply rooted notions of Biblical faith: the idea of the creation and fall of man. If this has to be given up, what becomes of the birth and redemption of Christ ? What becomes of the inspiration of the Bible, or even its value as an historical record ? The ultimate issue is scarcely doubtful, however, and we have only to look back at the storm of controversy which was raised by such books as Lyell's "Geology", Darwin's "Descent of Man", or Chambers' "Vestiges of Creation"; and note with what complacency these and similar books are now regarded, to be convinced that science must win the day. Already the foremost thinkers, the wisest men in the Church, are endeavouring to modify the accepted interpretation of the Bible, in order to bring it into harmony with the overwhelming weight of scientific evidence. Alas for the apologists ! they yield the ground inch by inch, but slowly and surely the wave of advancing knowledge is obliterating the little sand-heaps which they raise in the hope of staying the tide. Science has come to teach much more than an isolated knowledge of matter and its properties. By its inductive methods it has arrived at certain generalizations, at certain conceptions of the operation of universal law, which strike at the very root of the cherished ideas of religion respecting divine interference and revelation. It strikes at the whole record of the Old Testament, so far as that relates in an exoteric form the origin and progress of the race towards divine knowledge, by a series of divine manifestations and interventions. It strikes at the miraculous in the New as well as in the Old Testament. It asserts that the laws of nature never have been, and never will be, broken. It extends to the remotest time, and to the most distant regions of space, the laws and principles which are found to condition us on this earth. It asserts the unity of the Cosmos, the operation of the same laws in both small and great, and the absolute unchangeable-ness and reliability of these laws. Looking back, it traces the present order to a pre-existing one, and that again to an earlier one, an endless sequence of cause and effect, but through all the self-same laws in operation as those which we find at the present day. Looking forward, the same view presents itself. Time is but a conception of our brain, something inherent in our mental constitution. Nature knows no time. She is the same yesterday, today, and forever. Our little span of life is great in comparison with the life of the lower orders, some of which complete their term in a few moments, yet our longest span is as naught compared with the life of the species, and that, again is but a passing phase — the whole history of our globe but a raindrop falling into the ocean of eternity.

What name shall we give to these conceptions of science ? Shall we call them Atheism, Materialism, Agnosticism, or do they admit of Deism or Pantheism ? Well, let them be any one or all of these, they exist for the time being as *forms*, representative of various states of knowledge or consciousness of the human mind relative to the universal mind, relative to absolute truth, for absolute truth must include all its manifestations. In the mineral, vegetable, and animal kingdoms, we see that the principle of *life* manifested in thousands of forms, ever ascending the evolutionary scale from what we term *dead* matter to the highly organized and self-conscious animal called *man*. We do not see the transformation from unconscious or *dead* matter to organic structures, nor from the lower forms of these through all the intermediate grades of vegetable and animal up to the human race, for these processes take millions and millions of years, and according to the teachings of occult science are not effected on this globe only. But though the change takes place so slowly as to be imperceptible even to the most extended range of ordinary scientific investigation, yet we may apprehend that all the forms which we now see existing in the various kingdoms of nature are only temporary, partial and progressive manifestations of the *one life*, of that which underlies the form, and of which the form is an expression for the time being, representing a certain idea or state of consciousness.

In the same way with those higher aspects of consciousness which are manifested in the human mind. In no two minds does consciousness exist in absolutely the same degree, any more than two leaves of a tree are exactly alike. Collectively we are able to say that the leaves belong to the same tree or species, and also that a man belongs to a certain class, religion, or school of thought, each of which represents collectively a well-defined idea, or state of consciousness, relatively to that absolute principle or truth which each partially expresses.

Men are ever trying to reach this principle, it is the evolutionary power which prevents them from standing still, and from the time being, because they cannot estimate the forward movement, they fondly imagine that they have found it in some one or other of the *forms or systems* of religion of philosophy.

But the absolute truth must include every religion, every philosophy, and must show the connection and necessity of each. The man, therefore, who only recognises the reflection of truth in one religion, one philosophy, or one school of thought, by whatever *ism* it may be called, is still under the veil of *maya*, has still to learn that the same principle which manifests itself in the outward world in thousands of forms and species, in shapes of loveliest beauty as well as in deadly and hideous forms, manifests itself also in the human soul in corresponding and ever-varying phenomena.

Man is ever collecting from the elements of Nature and building around himself a concrete structure in which to centre his consciousness, until at last he loses sight altogether of the larger possibilities and nature of his real self, and takes that to be the only real which he has in pain and sorrow succeeded in centring around his personality. We find this illustrated in every phase of his existence, from the larger cycle of the descent of the spirit into matter during the Manvantara, to those smaller cycles which constitute each successive earth-life of the Ego. On the morning of each day, after the sleep and unconsciousness of night, the man awakes, and *necessity* compels him to take up his task at the point at which he left it yesterday. So after the sleep of death, *Karma* becomes active, and the Ego begins to construct a physical body in which it may function and manifest in that *form* which corresponds to its real character or state of consciousness. The child is spiritual, pure, innocent, free; lives half in heaven and half on earth, for the spirit is not yet wholly centred in the physical organization. We watch the growth from childhood to manhood; what becomes of the innocence, the purity, the spirituality? how often do we mourn the loss of these! The veil of the illusion of the senses is complete: the child becomes a man, and loses sight altogether of his higher self, his spiritual nature, or retains it only as a vague aspiration which finds an expression in religious emotion. He commences on a still lower plane, the same process of accretion, accumulation and self-centralization which brought him to earth, and spends his energies, his divine powers, in the gratification of the senses, or the acquisition of wealth, fame, or power; calling these *his own*, and centring in them his whole life and consciousness. Truly did Christ say that a rich man should hardly enter the kingdom of heaven, and that to do so we must become as little children.

It is not that either wealth or fame are in themselves evil, but simply the desire for them which leads men to expend their life forces on that which is illusory and transitory, and which blinds them to the higher possibilities of their nature, and hinders the development of the real, the divine man.

Science endeavours to connect all the phenomena of the universe in one harmonious whole, and to show the inter-dependence and co-relation of every part, and though she has only succeeded in doing this to a very limited extent on the physical plane merely, yet it is fundamental with her that not one atom exists except as an integral and necessary part of the whole, and not one form of life is manifested apart from that universal principle which is active in everything that lives and moves and has its being.

And now what is required is that this principle of unity shall be extended so as to embrace the higher psychical and spiritual aspects of our nature, so as to embrace that inner consciousness of our relation to a higher and unseen world which men in all ages have sought to express in a thousand different ways. What is required is a knowledge of the co-relation of the physical with the spiritual, a bold step forward from matter to spirit, from the seen to the unseen, from the known to the unknown.

Religion is a witness in each individual heart to the possibilities and reality of the unseen universe, and just as men's conceptions of the material world have varied from age to age, and assumed now one form, now another, so have his conceptions of the world of spirit varied and found expression in numberless forms of worship and superstition.

But religion has hitherto drawn a sharp line of demarcation between the natural and the supernatural, between the material and the spiritual. With regard to the spiritual she claims a supernatural revelation, and in so far as each and every religion lays claim in a special sense to such a revelation, there must exist an antagonism between one religion and another in their lower, outward, or exoteric aspect. But that no line of demarcation really exists, such as religion claims, is readily apprehended when we see how science is ever pushing this imaginary line further and further back, is ever carrying *natural* law further and further into those shadowy realms to which the mind of man relegates those personal activities with which he invests his conceptions of a Deity. Darkness and ignorance co-exist with superstition and fear; knowledge and light bring truth and love.

Does God retreat as science advances, or is he the same yesterday, today, and forever ? To what region can we now relegate those personal activities of the Deity, those *miracles* with which the Old and New Testaments are crammed ? If these are to stand in their literal, external, and narrative form, it rests with those who uphold them, with the church, to bring them into harmony with what we now know respecting the operation of natural laws. But if the first chapter of Genesis, and the Mosaic record of the dealings of Jehovah with his chosen people are to be considered as myths, allegories and fables, what becomes of the connection between the Old and the New Testaments ? If the foundations are taken away, what becomes of the superstructure ?

Although the church as a body still clings to the text of the Bible, there are those in her ranks who perceive the hopelessness of doing so, and who endeavour to meet the enlightenment and science of the age by a corresponding advance. Within the Church, as well as outside of it, the old beliefs are crumbling to dust before the advancing tide of knowledge, which is slowly, but surely, pushing the supernatural further and further back.

And now men no longer believe in the *super*-natural at all, and they reject all and every religion that is based upon supernatural claims. And yet — strange paradox — while supernatural religion is losing its hold on men's minds, supernatural science — if we may use such a term for the time being — is taking possession of the field. While men are casting off the marvellous on which they have hitherto based their conceptions of Deity, there is opening up before them a still more marvellous region, and phenomena which for the time being appear to be nothing more or less than miraculous in the very largest sense of that term. The literature of the day terms with the "occult". Spiritualism has its thousands of adherents who can testify to the reality of certain phenomena which are not produced by any known physical means. Science, for the time being, denies these manifestations *en masse*, for science is as dogmatic in her way as religion, but even science is now compelled to investigate them, and to testify to the reality of phenomena which she formerly denied. Mesmerism has been dubbed by another name, because science would not acknowledge Mesmer and his teachings, and so now it is called "hypnotism" and under this name has been subject to ample scientific demonstration. Thought-reading and clairvoyance have been attested by a learned and scientific body such as the Society for Psychical Research.. Even ghosts, which have hitherto been considered essentially supernatural, are receiving scientific attention, while works on alchemy, astrology, and palmistry abound.

Truly the supernatural is ever pressing in upon us, and if we drive it back in, one direction, it takes us by a flank movement. But supernaturalism is not necessarily superstition. Superstition implies ignorance and a dread of those powers of which we are ignorant. But now we must drop the term *supernatural*, for the supernatural is no longer a superstition, it is becoming a science.

Those who are acquainted with the teachings of the *Esoteric Doctrine* respecting the evolutionary cycles of the various races, will recognize how this state of things is being brought about in the present age. Man having passed the turning point, the lowest part of the cycle, and being now on the ascending arc, his whole being is becoming more spiritualized, and he is developing additional faculties which enable him to cognise certain things which are beyond the reach of the mere physical functions. But it is no longer with superstitious awe that he will regard the unknown region he is about to enter. With a knowledge of the unbroken sequence of cause and effect on the physical plane, and a reliance on the order and unity of natural law, he will be able to carry his knowledge and conceptions a stage further, and grasp the reality of the higher planes of existence which are not cognizable with the physical faculties, but which nevertheless are objective and real to those faculties (as yet but little known to the majority of men) which correspond with and find their expression on the higher planes. There is no sudden jump from the natural to the supernatural, from the sensuous to the supersensuous, from the physical to the spiritual. The spiritual world is not that which we enter at death: it is here, now, ever present, ever becoming; and if we are not cognizant of it, that is because our spiritual faculties are not developed, because we have no spiritual self-consciousness. Our consciousness is centred in our physical organs, and *matter* on the physical plane appears the only real.

There is no arbitrary line between time and eternity, between past, present, or future; neither is there any line of demarcation between the material and the spiritual. The aspects, laws, conditions, and phenomena of the one are the expression of similar laws conditioning the other.

Men are putting aside superstitious religion based upon supernaturalism. They are putting aside the Bible as a collection of fables and myths no longer tenable, and the question is whether in doing so they are making a progressive or a retrogressive step. It would appear that at first the step must be retrogressive; it is a smaller cycle within a larger one, and commences with a descending arc. The reaction from superstition leads to materialism, but this is only temporary.

And now, when men are demanding a larger knowledge and a deeper spiritual insight, there is discovered to them a possibility and source of knowledge and wisdom far surpassing their largest expectations. This knowledge is only new in the sense that it is now given to the world afresh and in a new form. In reality, it is as old as the hills, for it is the ancient "Secret Doctrine", or "Wisdom Religion", which has been the inheritance of the spiritual adepts and initiates in all ages. It does not supersede, but it gives a new meaning to old beliefs. It does not put aside the sacred books, but it is the true key and commentary to them, for it gives the real meaning of that which they express in allegory and fable.

From the first chapter of Genesis to the last chapter of Revelation, we may read the Bible without this key, and it will claim our superstitious reverence, and belief in its superhuman origin, or be rejected in the light of modern science and criticism. But when once we have apprehended that the Bible was written by men who *knew*, that it is a book of symbolism and not of history, that it contains the same teachings as the sacred books of other nations and races, only wrapped up in a different allegory; there no longer exists for us the necessity of regarding it either with superstitious reverence, or with incredulity; but it becomes to us a storehouse of knowledge which we may verify in a thousand ways, without waiting for an entry into the spirit-world through the gates of death.

It is no loss to cast away the supernaturalism of the Bible if we gain thereby that deeper knowledge which it contains, but which was never given to the world save in allegorical form, having generally, however, some slight historical basis. Is it any loss when we discover the true value and meaning of the fairy tales and romances which delighted our childhood? And if any ask why this knowledge should be so wrapped up that the real nature of it cannot be recognized without the key which the *Secret Doctrine* supplies, the answer is the same as that which we should give in reference to the fables which delight the childish mind. There are some things we cannot tell to a child in their plain meaning, and others which, if we did tell, he would not understand. The knowledge is there for him to possess in due time, but he must grow up to it, and must reach out to it with his own developed powers and will. Ah! but it is just here that we fail most to realise our position, to realise that we are but as the child to the man that will be. With a view of humanity extending over only a few thousand years at most, and of the individual confined to one brief life-time, how can it be otherwise? The *belief* that they will live again on this earth is too heavy a burden for most people; and did they really *know* it, they would be utterly crushed. How few there are who even truly realise for one moment that someday they must *die*. It is always *some day* with them, and even that *preparation* for death which they superstitiously believe to be necessary, is put off till the last moment. Then the priest is called in to do that which the man should have been doing for himself all his life-time. Truly did Christ say to his disciples, "I have many things to say unto you, but ye cannot bear them now". The Bible was written for men who were even more childish than we are, and if we think now that we have a claim to be told in somewhat plainer language what its real meaning is, well, — the key is now offered to the world. How many of those who should be most anxious for it will accept it? We are told that there are seven keys to unlock the sacred treasures, and that each key must be turned seven times; how many in this generation will raise their hand to the lock, and turn the first key once? Perhaps they will rather examine the key as a curious *forgery*, and even deny that there is any use for it at all.

Just as a deeper knowledge awaits the child when he shall have grown up to that stage where it is possible for him to lay hold of it, so does a deeper knowledge await the human race and the individual when they shall have reached that stage of evolution, that state of consciousness, which makes it possible for them to apprehend it. Then let the key be offered to them, and instinctively they know the use of it. Behold! the truth stands revealed to the inner man, where previously only the form was perceived on the outer plane.

But there is no finality. Deeper and deeper shall we penetrate, but the infinite is ever before us. Those who have gone the furthest realise this the best. There is always an ideal *beyond*. Our greatest geniuses, poets, painters, philosophers, are those who know best that they have but touched the border land of that in which they excel far beyond all their fellows. And if this be true, where is that finality, that arbitrary line which every religion draws, and refuses to believe that others have the right or the power to step over it except to their own destruction ? Every religion draws the line in a different place, and this fact alone should be sufficient to convince us that there is no one true religion, but that each represents a certain stage in the evolutionary cycle, and that even the highest and best, whichever that may be, must necessarily be only a partial revelation; while the highest and most exalted conceptions of a Deity must not merely fall far short of the actual truth, but be subject to the same kind of change that takes place in the relationship of the child to his father, when the child becomes a man, and no longer regards the father as the highest embodiment of wisdom, knowledge and authority.

Many a child has asked "Who made us" ? and when he is told that it was God, he asks, "Who made God?" It is not merely one veil — that of the flesh — which hides from us the source of our being. There is not one inner man merely, but many. Physical man is the outermost shell which has to be periodically cast off and periodically renewed, until the next inner man has developed sufficiently to live and act consciously without it. The faculties of this next inner man are beginning to be understood in this generation, and the possibility of exercising them on a plane which is just once removed from that of our physical senses is becoming a matter of *scientific* knowledge. But it is not here that we shall find those lines by which religion seeks to limit the illimitable, or those personal attributes with which she endeavours to invest the Deity.

"As in Adam all die, even so in Christ shall all be made alive again". Yea, truly; only then we must know who Adam and Christ really represent. The one is not the first man who was *created* some 6,000 years ago; neither is the other that which the Church conceives at the present time. Let those who wish to know use the key.

If men are unconscious of the possibility, existence, or necessity, of a deeper knowledge of the Bible than they now possess, they will reject the key that is offered to them, simply because they cannot recognise that it is a key, or that there is anything to open. The material world of sense, form, and colour is the most real thing to us; we cannot conceive of any other aspect of those things with which we are so familiar, and to a knowledge of the real essence of which this very familiarity is the greatest impediment. And yet, one step forward in the development of our faculties, and our conceptions of *matter* become totally altered; for matter is no longer solid and tangible; it is no longer that by which we are conditioned. It does not cease to exist, but our previous conceptions of it are found to be merely the illusions of the senses, the necessary result of a certain state of our consciousness. How reluctant men are to lose their hold of the solid and tangible, and how eagerly they cling to life on the physical plane! And so it is also with the forms in which they clothe their conceptions of the spiritual activities of the universe.

In their lowest aspect they are grossly material. We send missionaries to the poor heathen to show them a better way, a more spiritual light. Are there no missionaries required for *Christian* England ? Are not men asking on every side for more light, more knowledge, more truth than the church can give them ? When they ask for bread, does not the church offer a stone ? Is not the complaint everywhere heard that the church is losing its hold upon the masses, while those who lead the way in literature, science, or art, for the most part unhesitatingly reject her teachings ? It is not that the Gospel of Christ has ceased to be a power unto salvation for thousands of souls. Far be it from us to say that the church has no message for poor, ignorant, sinful man; only let her not conceive that those forms in which she wraps up the truth, and in which she now presents it to the world, have any finality, solidity, or permanence. Her own history during the present century will negative this view. We hear something of *advanced* views of Christianity in the church, but even the most *advanced* conceptions may be found in a new light to be as illusory as are our present conceptions of the constitution of *matter*, as it exists in relation to our physical senses.

If we wish to convey some idea to the mind of a child, or an ignorant person, we must bring the idea down to the level of his intellectual powers, and present it to him in some suitable form. The human race, as a whole, are but children in spiritual knowledge and power, but there are those who have advanced far beyond the limits which it is possible for us even to imagine, and who from time to time have given to the world in such manner as it was possible to do so, that higher knowledge which they have acquired. They are the "Elder Brothers" of the race.

And now in the present century they have given us a key that we may unlock some of those treasures, some of those deeper mysteries of our being which have become thickly encrusted with the ecclesiastical accumulations of centuries, and were in danger of becoming even further removed from our consciousness in an age of materialism and scepticism.

Theosophical teachings are based upon the larger view of humanity which we are enabled to take by reason of that knowledge of the origin, history and destiny of the race which the "Esoteric Doctrine" reveals. Theosophy is not *a* religion, it is rather *Religion* itself, for it embraces every religion. Those who cannot advance to that point where it becomes possible to form a generalization which shall include every religion as a manifestation of one universal principle, will probably reject Theosophical teachings; but others will find in them the possibility of uniting that which is apparently contradictory and antagonistic in the exoteric forms in which religion presents itself at different times, in every country and race, and in the human heart and consciousness.

WHAT IS THE THEOSOPHICAL SOCIETY?

AN OPINION IN REGARD TO WHAT IT OUGHT TO BE

I am often asked by strangers who have heard some account of the doings of the Theosophists: — What is the Theosophical Society and what is its purpose ? Some believe it to be a sect, in which no opinion is suffered to exist unless it is first sanctioned by certain "headquarters" or "Boards of Control"; others believe it to be a school for Occultism and Witchcraft; others think that it is a new form of Buddhism, coming under some disguise to overthrow Christianity, while some of those who do not belong to the Christian Church suspect it of being an effort to spread Christian Doctrines among them by clothing them in some new and more acceptable form. Nearly every one of such enquirers sees in the T.S. only a bugbear, and there are all sorts of opinions, except the right one, prevailing about it.

To all such objections I can only answer by showing the printed "Rules of the Theosophical Society", where, under the head "Objects of the Society", it says: — "The Society represents no particular religious creed, interferes with no man's caste, is entirely unsectarian", and includes professors of all faiths". This sounds so beautiful that people who have been accustomed all their life to cling to creeds and dogmas and "recognised authorities" are unable to believe that it can be true. Moreover, the objectors have heard of "Boards of Control", of "Presidential Orders", of "Official Organs", etc., and all these things have such an air of sectarianism that they seem to be hardly compatible with the spirit of freedom so loudly proclaimed by the T.S. It is asked:— What has a " Board of Control" to control ? Who enforces obedience to the Presidential Orders ? Does the Official Organ promulgate the dogmas of the sect ? And, if not, what then is the use of these things ? It seems, therefore, time that we should once more consider what the T.S. is, or what it ought to be. It must be plain to every lover of the truth that, however great the progress may be which modern civilisation has made with regard to the material and temporal welfare of man, the world is still far from having attained physical, intellectual, moral, and spiritual perfection. Disease and crime, suffering and death, poverty, tyranny and ignorance are still in existence, and although there are many organised bodies whose purpose it is to do good and to cure the ills of humanity, still the majority of such bodies are hampered to a certain extent by old beliefs, usages, creeds and superstitions, and their activity is not sufficiently free, because their opinions are not free; they may benefit a certain class of humanity, but not all mankind; they know perhaps a part of the truth, but not all of it; their charity extends over a small circle, but not over the whole world. The root of all evil is ignorance, with its children, superstition, fear, crime and disease; and the only remedy against ignorance is to spread the knowledge of truth.

There have been at all times men and societies willing to spread that which they believe to be the truth by all means which were at their command, whether fair or foul; there have been people ready to force their opinions in regard to the truth upon others, by the power of the sword and fagot, the rack and the fire; but the truth cannot spread in this manner. Real knowledge of the good, the beautiful, and the true can only be attained by obtaining the knowledge of self, and the knowledge of self must grow to every individual in the course of his development. It can no more be implanted by others or be forced upon another than a tree can be made to grow by pulling its trunk. The object of the true Theosophist is, therefore, to attain self-knowledge, and to employ the knowledge which he possesses for the purpose of accomplishing the greatest good.

There is, perhaps, not a single country upon the face of the earth in which may not be found a number of persons who desire to obtain self-knowledge, to find the truth by means of a free and unrestricted investigation, and to employ their knowledge for the benefit of humanity. There are persons who desire to see true progress in place of stagnation, knowledge in the place of accepted but still dubious opinions, wisdom in the place of sophistry, universal love and benevolence in the place o selfishness. Such men and women may be found here and there, and each one acts in the way he considers best. Some work by means of the school, others by means of the pulpit; some teach science, others influence a sense of the beautiful and true by their works of art, others speak the powerful language of music; but the most advanced of these give an example to others by their own Christlike conduct in the affairs of everyday life.

The great majority of such persons, interested in the welfare of humanity, live isolated, though they may be residing in crowded cities: for they find few who share their mode of feeling and thought, and who have identical objects in view. They are often living in communities where little except selfishness, the greed for money-making, or perhaps bigotry and superstition, are found, they are isolated and without the support of those who sympathise with their ideas; for although one universal principle unites all those who have the same object in view, still their persons are unknown to each other, and they seldom find means for mutual intercourse and exchange of thought.

Now let us suppose that in each country a centre of communication were to be established, by means of which such persons could come into contact with each other, and that at each such centre a journal or newspaper .were to be established, by means of which such persons could exchange their thoughts — not a centre from which supreme wisdom was to be dispensed, and from whence dogmas were to be doled out for the unthinking believers, but a centre through which the thought of the members of the society could freely flow — and we should then have an ideal "Theosophical Society". Such a centre would resemble a central telephone station, to which all the different wires extend, and it would require a trustworthy servant at the office to connect the wires and attend to the external business connected with the affairs of the offices; but if such a " telephonic operator" should attempt to interfere with the messages running over the wires, and to assume an authority to say what kinds of opinions should be wired and what messages should be suppressed: if he were to assume the *role* of a dictator, and permit only such messages to pass over the wires as would be in harmony with his own ideas, then the object of the centre of communication would come to nought, we should again have Papal dictates and Presidential orders in the place of liberty of thought and speech, and there would be an end of the object and purpose of the Society.

But, on the other hand, if every unripe mind were to be permitted to have its effusions printed at the expense of the Society, and to teach things which, perhaps a few months afterwards, having learned to know better, he would be sorry to think had ever seen the light, such a proceeding would throw discredit upon the Society, and be, moreover, altogether impracticable.

Our "telephone operator" should, therefore, be a man possessed of the greatest circumspection and discrimination; and while he should never interfere with the expression of any opinion, no matter how much opposed to his own, he should, at the same time, be permitted to cut down the messages sent over his wires to certain limits, and to present them, if necessary, in a more suitable form.

As regards the liberty of speech, it would be an absurdity if such a Society were to attempt to prescribe to any of its members what kind of opinions or dogmas he should express, because, whatever opinions he may pronounce, they could never be regarded as the opinions of the Society as a whole; for the Society, as such, "represents no particular creed", and "is entirely unsectarian". If, in spite of this solemn assertion, anyone chooses to believe that the opinions publicly expressed by a member of the Society represent the creed of the Society, such an unfortunate circumstance can only be deplored, but will do no serious harm. On the other hand, if "a President" or "Board of Control" should attempt to preside over more important things than merely over the meetings of the members, and if a "Board of Control" should attempt to control the conscience and opinions of the members, instead of merely exercising its control over the external affairs of the Society; and if an "official organ" should attempt to postulate what ought and what ought not to be believed by members of the Society, such a proceeding would be in direct opposition to the spirit, the object, and the purpose of that Society, and in contradiction to the principles on which it was founded; and while it should be the object of every lover of truth to assist the growth of a true "Theosophical Society", and to maintain its purity of principle, it should also be his aim to suffocate in the germ, everything that is opposed to liberty and freedom of speech.

www.ingramcontent.com/pod-product-compliance
Lightning Source LLC
LaVergne TN
LVHW041500070426
835507LV00009B/713